CONTENTS

SHETLAND MUSEUM

A LIVING MUSEUM, A LIVING HERITAGE

Welcome to Shetland Museum and Archives – the islands' cultural, heritage and social hub – a landmark on the Lerwick waterfront.

Discover the islands' many secrets through the exhibits and displays, and take a look in the boat-shed where you can see demonstrations of traditional boat-building skills. Also, be sure to visit Da Gadderie, the museum's temporary exhibition gallery that hosts a diverse range of exhibitions throughout the year.

For more in-depth study don't miss out on the Archives, where you can delve into the written and spoken word of Shetland's past.

After all that, relax in the Hay's Dock Café Restaurant, and enjoy the superb cuisine and panoramic views.

The Building

Her Majesty The Queen of Norway and Their Royal Highnesses the Duke and Duchess of Rothesay opened Shetland Museum and Archives at Hay's Dock on 31st May 2007. This marked a historic event - the Museum and Archives' rich collections being brought together for the first time, to tell a powerful story.

Today's Shetland is celebrated throughout the building. Areas and details were created by local craftspeople and artists, and where possible locally recycled materials have been incorporated.

However, this is more than a building. Shetland Museum and Archives is a focus for community events, study and learning. In addition to the impressive main galleries and archive facilities, the learning room and auditorium provide additional spaces for community events and activities.

The Galleries

The galleries are split over two floors; the Lower Gallery concentrates on the period up to 1800, while the Upper Gallery covers the years from 1800 to present day.

As you enter the Lower Gallery the clock is turned back to tell some of Shetland's earliest stories. Walk through to learn about Shetland in the Ice Age, and as time progressed how people have lived and survived in the islands. Evocative recordings of folklore and customs, music and dialect will accompany you on your journey.

AND ARCHIVES

You then enter the impressive three-storey Boat Hall, with displays of historic boats suspended from the ceiling. Viewing platforms provide an opportunity to see the boats from stunning angles.

The Upper Gallery goes on to reveal how from 1800 the islands were opened up to outside influences, and how Shetlanders' lives were transformed. It features displays on culture and trade, and also houses displays of the museum's internationally important textiles collection.

The Archives

The Archives searchroom is a haven of peace in a busy building. Here you can research the history of your family or house, read dozens of books and newspapers about Shetland's history, and listen to recordings of Shetlanders past and present.

Your visit

Today's visit to the Shetland Museum and Archives is just the start of your journey of discovery into the islands' heritage. Here you will find details of the network of smaller museums, and other interesting buildings and sites to visit across Shetland.

Enjoy your journey through Shetland's past and present – a fascinating tale, stunningly told.

Credits

For assistance with text: Charlie Simpson and Richard Whitaker.
For assistance with illustrations: Alan Mckay.
For assistance with photography: Davy Cooper, Billy Fox, Mark Sinclair, Didier Piquer, Brydon Thomason and Malcolm Younger – please see page 41 for full credits.

HAY'S DOCK

The Shetland Museum and Archives occupies the last area of original dock on the Lerwick waterfront.

Hay's Dock dates from 1822. It was constructed by the firm of Hay & Ogilvy, and soon became one of the busiest spots in Lerwick.

The firm's leading light was William Hay (1787-1858), who was born into a family of traders and smugglers. He entered into a partnership with his wife's father and brothers in 1822.

Seals and wading birds can be seen in the dock.

The firm invested in the herring fishery, and vessels landed the catches for curing at their Freefield base.

As trade grew, the Freefield site boomed. Quays, docks, a shipyard, warehouses and workshops sprang up, together with stores for salt, housing for tradesmen, warehouses for provisions, cooperages, smithies, a sawmill and ship chandler.

The shipyard built a number of herring drifters, cod smacks, trading schooners and the barque *North Briton*, the largest vessel ever built in Shetland. One visitor described the company's great stores, building yard and curing houses as "an immense concern, containing within itself the means and materials of every kind of work, and rather resembled a small self-contained colony than a private establishment, so numerous and complete are its docks and harbours, ships, quays and other conveniences."

By 1839, Hay & Ogilvy was prosperous, owning or managing 100 fishing vessels. But the prosperity didn't last. A series of poor fishing seasons and bad harvests drained its resources, and mismanagement of the Shetland Bank, in which the Hays and Ogilvys were majority shareholders, made things worse. By 1842 both the company and the bank were declared bankrupt.

William Hay and his sons formed Hay & Company in 1842, and the new firm quickly established itself as Shetland's main importer and exporter, trading as fish curers, factors, wholesalers and retailers with branches across the isles. The shipyard too was back in business and built many boats, from small "fourareens" to the 67-foot Fifie *Swan* in 1900.

The sail drifter Oriental *hauled up at Hay's Dock in the 1890s.*

Steam drifters crowd in around Freefield and the North Ness during the 1920s.

Later the dock became the base for Lerwick's fleet of small whitefish boats, and some of the quays were used for timber storage. Until 1980 almost all of Shetland's timber, coal, cement and building materials came through the sawmill and stores at Freefield.

Today Hay's Dock, beautifully restored, is the site for the Shetland Museum and Archives. The dock is now home to several art works, and the propeller from the stricken ocean liner *Oceanic*, lost off the island of Foula in 1914.

By the 1970s Hay's Dock was a home to the growing fleet of local pleasure craft.

THE BOATSHED

When Hay & Company took over Freefield in 1844, they built a boatshed at the head of the slipway. Until then, only small open boats could be built indoors.

The wooden boatshed made building more efficient, and less affected by bad weather and poor daylight. Together with the summer herring curing business, it also provided year-round employment in skilled trades serving the fishing industry. The boatshed became the hub of the company's operation since the boats built there caught the herring that were cured and exported. The present shed, from about 1900, is on the same site.

To keep the sheds in business, timber and spars, ironwork, cordage, nails, sailcloth and paint had to be imported. Shipwrights, carpenters, sawyers, blacksmiths, sail makers, riggers and labourers built the boats that, in turn, provided work for coopers, gutters, carters and more labourers.

David Leask was the boatshed foreman for more than 40 years, and supervised the building of his biggest and last creation, the Fifie *Swan*, in 1900. John Shewan followed him, creating many craft, including the *Maggie Helen* (now *Loki*) in 1904 and the motor-powered *Venture* in 1909.

Boatbuilding slowed down dramatically after the First World War, although repairs kept its tradesmen busy. Through the 1930s, Shetland's RNLI lifeboats were overhauled annually in the shed.

The Loki *back in the boatsheds for restoration, over 100 years after being built in the same place.*

Robbie Tait and Jack Duncan at work on a sixareen based on the museum's sixareen Industry.

Up Helly Aa longships were built in the boatshed until 1939. After the war, the shed fell silent and was used mainly as a timber store and for small boat repair work over the next 50 years.

With the arrival of the Shetland Museum and Archives building, the boatshed is busy once more. After extensive renovation, it now provides the perfect environment for visitors to witness painstaking boat restoration and boat-building skills close at hand.

The boatshed provides plenty of space for boat building and maintenance.

ARCHIVES

Researchers use the Archives to make discoveries about the history of Shetland. The collection contains all kinds of documents, books and sound recordings. It covers a large range of specialist areas including textiles, fishing and maritime history, music, and natural history.

The oldest document dates back to 1490, and new records are being acquired all the time.

Here are some examples of the records kept in the Archives:

● Records of Shetland Islands Council (from 1975 onwards) and its predecessors (1750s-1974), and records of Lerwick Town Council (1818-1974)

NOTICE.
At 4 o'clock P.M.
TO-MORROW
(FRIDAY, 18th curt.),
THE ESQUIMAUX
URIO STAWANJO,
At present in Lerwick, will Weather permitting, give an
EXHIBITION
IN HIS
KAYAK
In the Harbour.
And in the Evening, at 8 o'clock, he will appear in the
TOWN HALL
AND GIVE A
PERFORMANCE,
CONSISTING OF NATIVE SONGS & DANCES.
Captain ADAMS, of the ss. Maud, will give a short Lecture upon the Habits and Customs of the Natives of Greenland.
Sheriff MACKENZIE in the Chair
ADMISSION TO THE HALL, SIXPENCE EACH.

Poster advertising the visit of an Inuit in 1887.

● Papers of Lerwick Sheriff Court (1490 onwards) and other legal and police records
● Records of the Church of Scotland and other denominations (1675 onwards)
● Customs and Excise records (1790 onwards) including detailed fishing boat registers
● Records of individuals, estates and societies (1520s onwards).

The Archives also look after:
● Oral history tapes and transcripts
● Biggest collection of Shetland books, pamphlets, newspapers and journals anywhere
● Maps and plans
● Microfilm of old parish registers and censuses, newspapers and other documents.

The court records and legal and police records give details of crimes, suspected crimes, and civil cases such as land disputes, bankruptcies and debts.

A reader in the searchroom uses the extensive collection of microfilmed resources.

Church records include kirk session minutes with cases of slander, swearing, drunkenness, accounts of those who did not observe the sabbath, illegitimacy, adultery and fornication. The minutes also have information about help given to poor people. The church records also include some registers of births, marriages, and deaths.

Local authority records contain information about roads, education, poor relief, housing, health, law and order, leisure, and the many other areas that councils were involved in.

The microfilm section includes parish registers from the 1600s onwards, and censuses from 1841. There is a complete series of both *The Shetland Times* and *Shetland News*, and Orkney and Caithness newspapers which were on the scene before newspapers were published in Shetland.

The large sound archive collection includes oral history recordings, music and folklore and the BBC Radio Shetland sound archive.

These sources can be used to help build a family tree, to study the history of a community, an industry or to help us learn more about any aspect of Shetland's history.

One of the public art works in the searchroom. Dr Mike MacDonnell's "Diaspora" portrays emigration from Shetland.

Catalogues for all the collections are available in the Archives, where people can come to read the documents or listen to the recordings.

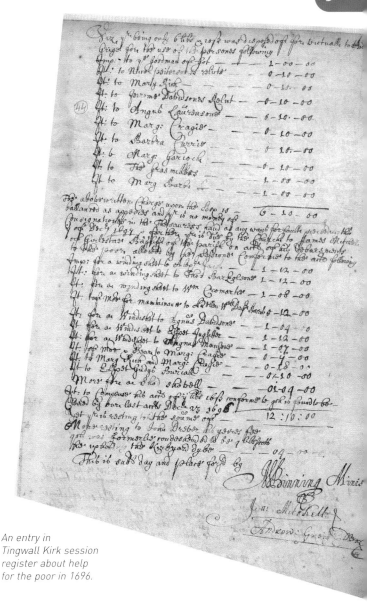

An entry in Tingwall Kirk session register about help for the poor in 1696.

Access to the records is free of charge, and staff are always on hand to help.

There are more than 100,000 documents housed in a special store, which keeps them secure and safe from the risk of fire, flooding and other damage.

The photographic archive of more than 70,000 images showing all aspects of Shetland life is available on the website.

EARLY BEGINNINGS

Shetland has been on a long, exciting journey over millions of years. Travelling on vast landmasses, known as tectonic plates, it has moved from near the South Pole to where it is today.

Almost three billion years ago Shetland and Scotland were part of the same continent as North America, but the continents slowly moved apart as they drifted across the world. Shetland and Scotland were eventually left on the European side of the Atlantic Ocean.

Eshaness cliffs - one of Shetland's most popular beauty spots, but few visitors experience the cliffs in the teeth of a force 9 storm.

Today Shetland is as close to the North Pole as Alaska or Greenland, but its climate is milder than these sub-Arctic regions. The North Atlantic Current brings warm water from the Gulf of Mexico, keeping the sea free of ice all year.

Shetland's dramatic and varied landscape was formed over millions of years from volcanic eruptions, deserts and colossal moving land masses. Later erosion by wind, water, ice and the sea then shaped the landscape.

At the end of the last ice age Shetland was probably a barren, rocky wilderness but animals, plants and insects soon began to colonise the islands. They arrived by wind and sea, or hitched a lift with birds.

Microscopic lichen, fungi, moss and fern spores were blown to Shetland by the wind and grew into the first plants to inhabit the bare rocks. Seeds soon began to flourish in a soil formed from droppings and plant matter. Today Shetland has a great diversity of plants and wildlife, some of them unique to the islands.

Komatiite is rare: south-west Africa is the nearest place you could find some more. In Shetland we find it in the South Mainland, marking the place where the continents split apart about 600 million years ago.

WORLD | **SHETLAND**

YEARS AGO

The last ice age was only about 10,000 years ago, and formed ice over Shetland up to 800 metres thick. A young visitor feels the ice rumbling across the rock.

3 billion - Rocks on which Shetland sits were formed. Shetland lay on the edge of the same continent as North America

600 million - Shetland had almost reached the South Pole but was beginning to drift northwards again

First plants appeared - **430 million**

England and Scotland - **400 million** were united geologically for the first time

400 million - Shetland was a desert lying just south of the equator. America, with Shetland attached, collided with Scandinavia, then Europe

Were otters Shetland's first land animals?

300 million - As Shetland moved north across the equator, seawater flooded into the area which is now the North Sea

Age of the dinosaurs - **150 million**

Shetland and Scotland - **60 million** remained on the European side and were separated from America by a spreading Atlantic Ocean

60 million - Shetland drifted towards its present position and the continent split again

Neanderthal people - **350,000** appeared in Europe

The islands are made up of a wide variety of rocks and minerals including ignimbrite, felsite, steatite, chromite, copper, magnetite, quartz and limestone. When people first came to Shetland almost six thousand years ago they began to use rocks and minerals to make tools and build shelters.

The last ice age began - **25,000** and lasted 15,000 years

25,000 - The ice sheet over Shetland during this time may have been between 500 and 800 metres in depth and covered all of Shetland's major hills

The geologist Samuel Hibbert examined these glacial erractics in 1818.

The climate warmed up - **9,000** and allowed woodlands to spread across Europe

9,000 - Shetland's woods included aspen, birch, hazel, rowan and willow

Temperatures cooled and a - **8,000** period of higher rainfall began

8,000 - Vegetation gradually changed, with peat forming in many places

6,000 - Humans arrived and altered the landscape further through agricultural practices and settlement

Britain became an island - **5,000**

YEARS AGO

WORLD | **SHETLAND**

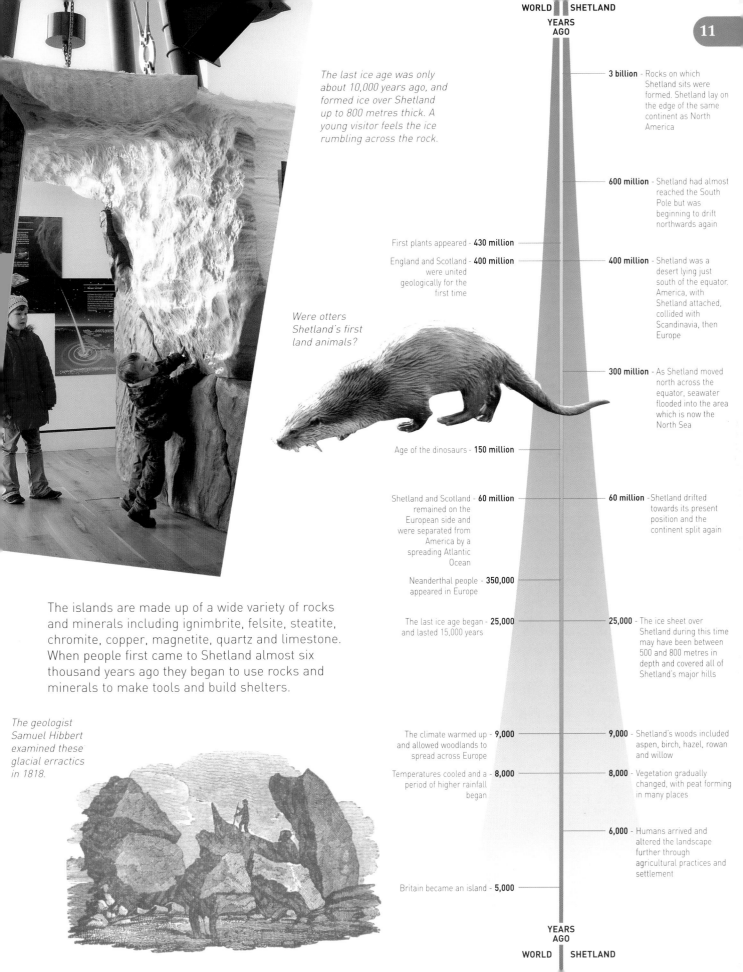

EARLY PEOPLE

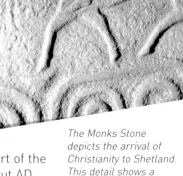

People have lived in Shetland for about 6000 years. Through all that time, the islands' unique challenges and resources have shaped the lives of their men, women and children.

When people first arrived in Shetland, the climate was warmer and drier than it is today. Settlers could live on the hills as well as the more fertile land near the shore. They relied on the natural resources they found nearby for food, housing, tools and clothes.

People shaped stones and bones into tools to help make fire, catch fish and work wood. The soil was cultivated to grow cereals, while plants were used to make rope. People later began to use metals – first bronze and later iron – to make tools, jewellery and weapons.

These arrowheads are very finely made from a very hard stone called quartz.

Early Shetlanders believed in an afterlife, and they placed everyday objects like tools and jewellery next to the bones in little chambered hilltop tombs. Later, when people moved from the hills to the coast, they buried their dead in stone boxes.

During the Iron Age, Shetlanders built large forts throughout the islands. We call these monuments brochs, and they were so massive that the ruins of them can still be seen. Often they were placed on the coast, to scan the seaways for enemies.

A Viking comb made from bone. Besides combs like this, others were used to remove lice.

Picts, a group of tribes in North Britain, eventually made their influence felt in the Northern Isles. Shetland became part of the Pictish kingdom. Until about AD 700 everyone who lived in Shetland was pagan, but sometime after that monks and priests from Scotland and Ireland introduced Christianity to the islands.

The sudden arrival of Viking raiders in Shetland, about AD 800, marked the beginning of a chaotic time that dramatically changed every aspect of island life. They sailed west from Norway by longship, and plundered the Pictish settlements, and removed all trace of local life and culture. Settlers followed, who set up house and became farmers and fishermen.

The islands became part of Norway. Shetlanders spoke a Scandinavian language, and all their traditions – their folklore and place names, building styles and farming methods – came from the east side of the North Sea.

The Monks Stone depicts the arrival of Christianity to Shetland. This detail shows a senior monk on his pony.

This large silver Viking brooch was found at Gulberwick. The small boy who found it was about to melt it for down for fishing weights, when he was stopped.

A 5000 year old face has been brought to life from a skull found in a mass burial at Dunrossness. The young woman was between 17-26 when she died.

> *"In the days of Harald Fairhair, king of Norway, certain Vikings, descended from the stock of that sturdiest of men, Earl Rognvald, crossing the Solund Sea with a large fleet, totally destroyed these people after stripping them of their long-established dwellings and made the islands subject to themselves."* Historia Norwegie | c.1160

Under Norwegian rule, Shetland had its own parliament and law court as part of the earldom of Orkney. The Vikings were pagans, but eventually they adopted Christian beliefs. In 1195 the king of Norway took Shetland directly under his control, following a rebellion.

In 1349 the relative calm of medieval Shetland was broken with the arrival of the Black Death. The plague ravaged populations across Europe and Shetland may have taken more than a century to recover.

Shetland's oldest surviving document dates from 1299. It is about a dispute on the island of Papa Stour.

In 1468-1469 Christian I, King of Norway and Denmark had to mortgage Shetland and Orkney to King James III of Scotland, as part of his daughter Margrethe's wedding dowry. That pledge was never redeemed, and Shetland became part of Scotland.

Although Shetlanders of the Middle Ages were Christians, they also used good luck charms, in an attempt to cure illnesses or injuries. This stone cup and horse were found together at Eshaness.

This fearsome Pictish dog-headed man was found carved on a stone at Mail in Cunningsburgh.

Butter was used to pay rents and taxes. It was kept fresh by burying it in the cold and damp peat moor.

Timeline

WORLD | BC | SHETLAND

- Wheel and plough invented - **c3500**
- Great Pyramid Age in - **c2700** Egypt began
- Acropolis of Athens built - **460**
- Great Wall of China started - **c200** — 0
- Roman invasion of Britain - **43**

- **c4000** - Shetland's first human inhabitants arrive. They lived near the shore and on the hillsides
- **c3200** - Earliest date for settlement at Sumburgh
- **c2200** - Stanydale "temple" built
- **c1700** - Climate became cooler and wetter
- **c200** - Last of brochs being built after 400 years of building
- **c700** - Priests and monks brought Christianity to the isles
- **c800** - Vikings colonised Shetland

- Norman conquest of - **1066** England
- First Crusade - **1095**

- **995** - The King of Norway declared his country Christian, and Christianity became the official religion of Shetland
- **1137** - Building started on St Magnus Cathedral, Orkney
- **1195** - Shetland detached from Earldom of Orkney and administered directly from Norway

- Black Death - **1349**

- **1349** - Black Death
- **c1450** - German merchants began to trade in Shetland
- **1468/9** - Christian I, King of Norway and Denmark, mortgaged Shetland and Orkney to King James III of Scotland as part of his daughter Margrethe's dowry

AD

HOME AND LAND

As Scottish influence over Shetland increased, local laws and customs were gradually replaced by Scots ones. Everyday tools and techniques remained unaltered.

During the first century of Scottish rule the islands saw little change. But in the 16th century the economy of northern Europe was growing again, and Shetland became attractive to Scottish landowners and merchants.

Scalloway in 1762; showing trading smacks at anchor.

They bought up estates, and islanders, some of whom had been freeholders, became tenants of the Scottish landowners. In the 1560s Scotland, including Shetland, broke away from the Catholic Church in favour of Protestantism, and the new church soon began to exert greater control over many aspects of peoples lives.

In 1593 Earl Patrick Stewart became Lord of Shetland. From his stronghold at Scalloway Castle he upset fellow landowners and their tenants, and made powerful enemies in Scotland. When he was beheaded for treason, in 1615, the landowners took control of the islands.

Shetlanders had traditionally traded with foreign merchants but around 1680 the islands' economy began to collapse. Foreign traders turned their backs on Shetland, and local merchant

landowners began to export fish to Germany. They forced their tenants to fish for them. For the next 170 years, commercial fishing dominated the Shetland economy and way of life.

Shetlanders were self-sufficient because they were isolated. Almost everything they used was made by themselves from local resources. In the home peat and fish oil were used for fires and lamps. People built their own houses with stone walls and roofs of straw and turf. With timber in short supply, driftwood and even wrecked ships were highly valued. Inside, houses were sparse with an open fire and basic homemade furniture. People made their own buildings, farm tools, and clothes as they had no money to pay craftsmen.

They did specific jobs at specific times, and the community worked together. A poor harvest meant less bread, less fodder, and less straw for thatching the roof. Animals were vital for wool and horn, as well as milk and meat.

All the land was divided between farming and grazing areas. Animals were moved to grazings, outside the dyke, during the summer growing season. After the harvest they came off the hills and often spent the harsh winter indoors. All Shetland livestock and crops were distinct local breeds, hardened to the local environment over many centuries. The Shetland cow, horse, pig, and sheep were smaller than other breeds.

Salt for cooking was kept in a saat cuddie. It hung near the hearth to keep the contents dry.

Wig stretcher used by the Cheyne family of Eshaness. Made by Johnny Williamson ("Joannie Notions") who invented a version of smallpox inoculation in the 1780's.

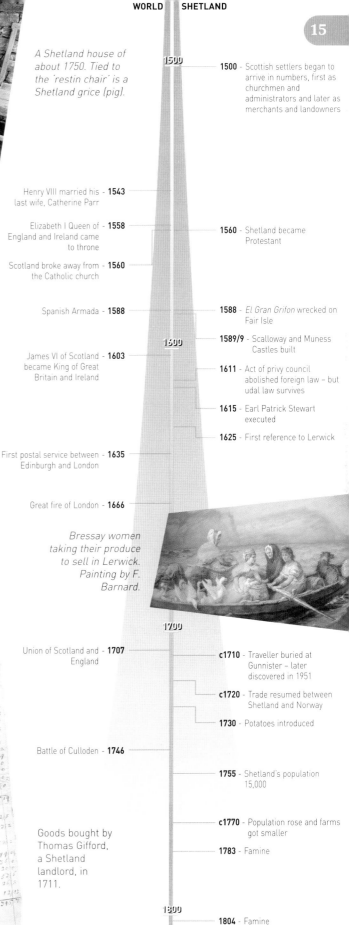

A Shetland house of about 1750. Tied to the 'restin chair' is a Shetland grice (pig).

Shetland's farmers grew barley, oats and kale and, from around 1730, potatoes too. In spring the land was fertilised, dug or ploughed and the seeds sown. Hay for winter fodder was cured, along with peat for fires.

The year was a cycle, based on the time the crops were growing. From May-October crops were growing and the livestock were on the hills. When the crops were harvested, winter would usually be spent threshing corn, grinding grain, repairing and renewing implements and domestic possessions, as well as spinning, knitting and weaving. Livestock stayed inside and survived on fodder for as long as it lasted.

Imported wooden containers were common in Shetland houses. Shetlanders took back Skovi kapps on voyages to the Baltic.

Farming changed the Shetland environment. It created a variety of new habitats that we value today because they support a wide range of plants and animals.

Bressay women taking their produce to sell in Lerwick. Painting by F. Barnard.

Goods bought by Thomas Gifford, a Shetland landlord, in 1711.

> **They make use of Barly-Bread, which appears to be fairer than their Oat-Bread, for their Barly they take to be the best Grain, it agreeing better with the ground than oats.**
> *Rev. John Brand | 1700*

WORLD | SHETLAND

1500
- **1500** – Scottish settlers began to arrive in numbers, first as churchmen and administrators and later as merchants and landowners

Henry VIII married his - **1543**
last wife, Catherine Parr

Elizabeth I Queen of - **1558**
England and Ireland came
to throne
- **1560** – Shetland became Protestant

Scotland broke away from - **1560**
the Catholic church

Spanish Armada - **1588**
- **1588** – *El Gran Grifon* wrecked on Fair Isle

1600
- **1589/9** – Scalloway and Muness Castles built

James VI of Scotland - **1603**
became King of Great
Britain and Ireland
- **1611** – Act of privy council abolished foreign law – but udal law survives

- **1615** – Earl Patrick Stewart executed

- **1625** – First reference to Lerwick

First postal service between - **1635**
Edinburgh and London

Great fire of London - **1666**

1700

Union of Scotland and - **1707**
England
- **c1710** – Traveller buried at Gunnister – later discovered in 1951

- **c1720** – Trade resumed between Shetland and Norway

- **1730** – Potatoes introduced

Battle of Culloden - **1746**

- **1755** – Shetland's population 15,000

- **c1770** – Population rose and farms got smaller

- **1783** – Famine

1800
- **1804** – Famine

WORLD | SHETLAND

CUSTOMS AND FOLKLORE

Gulsa [jaundice] was common condition. People took water from a stream in a kapp [bowl], and infused it with a special grass.

> *Folk have been led to think that their dialect, not being used by gentlefolks, must therefore be vulgar and better dropped. Naturally, customs and traditions follow.*
>
> *Jessie Saxby | 1932*

Shetlanders had many folk customs and beliefs. Through them they tried to explain the unknown, protect themselves from evil influences, and bring good luck into their lives. Traditions were passed from generation to generation through stories told by the fireside.

The islanders were Christian, but some beliefs and customs survived from Viking times. The Church was suspicious of these pagan traditions, which the Shetlanders combined with Christian ceremonies. Since most people believed the customs were important the church had little success in suppressing them and often they were carried out in secret.

Mythical creatures featured heavily in Shetland imaginations and stories. For example, the 'bridgi' spelt doom to seafarers, while the 'nyuggle' lured unlucky travellers into lochs.

After death the family dressed the body in special burial clothes called kistin claes, which were often kept in the bottom of a drawer or chest.

The apparently ordinary people known as finns secretly possessed extraordinary powers of invisibility and incredible strength, and could travel at great speed.

The most renowned creatures were the trows – fairy folk who lived underground during daylight. If provoked they could cause chaos around the farm. They prevented cows from giving milk, and stole babies and replaced them with sick trow children. The trows loved fiddle music, and many a fiddler was said to have been enticed underground to play for a night – only to find that when he surfaced again that a week, a year, or even a century had passed.

Superstition governed day-to-day activities on land and at sea. A special language was used by fisherman while at sea. They did not call everyday objects by their usual names, because they thought that would bring danger to their boat and its crew. People accused women, and sometimes men, of being witches. If a cow got ill or a boat sank people might blame a witch for casting a spell.

Music, song and dance played an important part in Shetland society, despite the influence of the Church. Although some old tunes survive today, the Scandinavian tradition of chanted ballads and

Pret Kendigaet Swaara Bleddick Sturken Kolkoom

On special occasions, during winter, youths would go 'skekkling'. They visited neighbours' houses in disguise, seeking gifts.

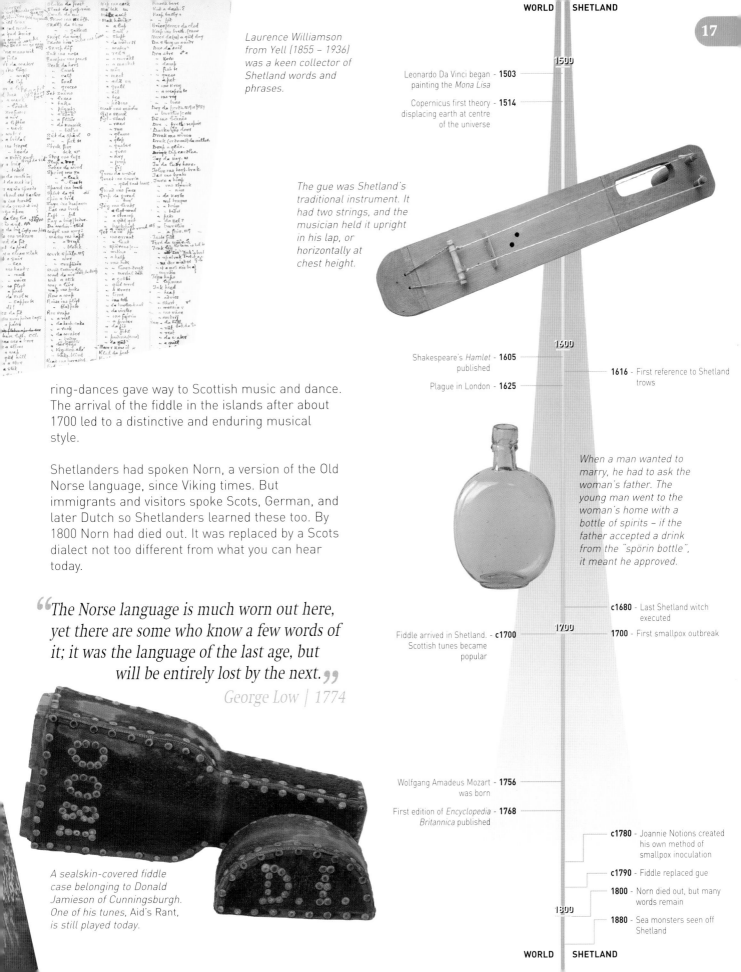

Laurence Williamson from Yell (1855 – 1936) was a keen collector of Shetland words and phrases.

The gue was Shetland's traditional instrument. It had two strings, and the musician held it upright in his lap, or horizontally at chest height.

WORLD   **SHETLAND**

1500

Leonardo Da Vinci began - **1503**
painting the *Mona Lisa*

Copernicus first theory - **1514**
displacing earth at centre
of the universe

1600

Shakespeare's *Hamlet* - **1605**
published

1616 - First reference to Shetland
trows

Plague in London - **1625**

When a man wanted to marry, he had to ask the woman's father. The young man went to the woman's home with a bottle of spirits – if the father accepted a drink from the "spörin bottle", it meant he approved.

ring-dances gave way to Scottish music and dance. The arrival of the fiddle in the islands after about 1700 led to a distinctive and enduring musical style.

Shetlanders had spoken Norn, a version of the Old Norse language, since Viking times. But immigrants and visitors spoke Scots, German, and later Dutch so Shetlanders learned these too. By 1800 Norn had died out. It was replaced by a Scots dialect not too different from what you can hear today.

c1680 - Last Shetland witch
executed

1700

Fiddle arrived in Shetland. - **c1700**
Scottish tunes became
popular

1700 - First smallpox outbreak

"The Norse language is much worn out here, yet there are some who know a few words of it; it was the language of the last age, but will be entirely lost by the next."

George Low | 1774

Wolfgang Amadeus Mozart - **1756**
was born

First edition of *Encyclopedia* - **1768**
Britannica published

c1780 - Joannie Notions created
his own method of
smallpox inoculation

c1790 - Fiddle replaced gue

1800 - Norn died out, but many
words remain

1800

1880 - Sea monsters seen off
Shetland

A sealskin-covered fiddle case belonging to Donald Jamieson of Cunningsburgh. One of his tunes, Aid's Rant, is still played today.

WORLD   **SHETLAND**

HARVEST FROM THE SEA

The sea was a plentiful resource for Shetland. It made life possible in the islands for the early settlers, and trade in fish products was the mainstay of Shetland's economy for 1,000 years.

The sea has always been an important resource for Shetlanders. Even when crops failed, it could be relied on to provide a harvest. At the same time, sea mammals and birds provided oil, bones and skin as well as meat. Seaweed fertilised the fields, and driftwood was useful for buildings and tools.

A pair of child's rivlins (shoes) made from sealskin.

Detail from a painting by R. H. Carter showing a 'caa' (whale hunt) in Dunrossness.

middle depth fish, such as cod. Fishermen would set lines on the seabed for deep swimmers like haddock, and they would spear flatfish in shallow areas. Shellfish were gathered for bait as well as for eating. Sea birds and their eggs, along with sea mammals, were also a significant source of food.

Some fish were eaten fresh, some were cured by salting and drying, while others were dried without salt. Lines of drying fish were an everyday sight, outdoors or above the hearth.

Trade developed because of Shetland's abundant fish stocks. From about 1450 German merchants set up trading booths all over the islands, and did business with Shetlanders from May to September.

Before 1800 people got a big proportion of their food from the sea. They needed a fine knowledge of fish habits, and of the environment, to get a good catch. Sillock (young coalfish), piltock (older coalfish) and saithe formed a staple year-round diet, together with fish liver and roes in season.

Different types of fish swim at different depths, so different methods were used to catch them. Surface swimmers, like piltocks, were caught by dragging a hand-line through the water. Pulling a hand-line up and down was the best method of catching

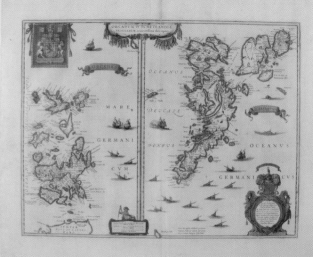

Map of Orkney and Shetland published in Amsterdam by Willem Blaeu in 1654.

A fisherman's hat in traditional Fair Isle patterns and colours.

From the booths they traded beer, flour, linen and pottery in return for fish. But by 1700, famine and war had ended their ventures.

Trade with Dutch herring fishermen began in the late sixteenth century. They lived on their boats and salted the fish onboard. Every year hundreds of busses (boats) and thousands of fishermen came. Local women sold them knitwear in exchange for money, gin or tobacco.

The growth of shipping trade, especially from the Netherlands to their colonies, brought large ships to Shetland waters. They didn't stop here, but sometimes they were wrecked. People prized items from their cargoes, and found their timbers and ropes useful too.

> **"**I inquired what they generally had for breakfast? They answered, "Piltocks." What for dinner? "Piltocks and cabbage." What for supper? "Piltocks." Some of them declared they had not tasted oat-meal or bread for five months.**"** *Patrick Neill | 1806*

Limpets were a common bait to use for inshore fishing. The pick was used to prise them from the rock and the shapper to pound them.

This pilk [fishing lure] is shaped like a small fish and has a polished surface to attract attention in the dark water.

The North Atlantic drift often brings leatherback turtles to Shetland. This female was found off Yell in 2000.

Timeline

- **c1450** - German merchants began to trade directly with Shetland
- **1500**
- Dutch East India company - **1602** formed
- **1600**
- Bananas first appeared in - **1633** British shops
- Anglo-Dutch wars began - **1650**
- **1627** - Dunkirk pirates attacked Shetland
- **1640** - Trade between Shetland and Norway began to die out
- **1664** - *Kennemerland* wrecked in Skerries
- **1700**
- **1707** - The last German merchants abandoned Shetland, local merchant lairds took over the fishery
- **c1720** - Development of the haaf fishery
- **1800**

Ground floor plan

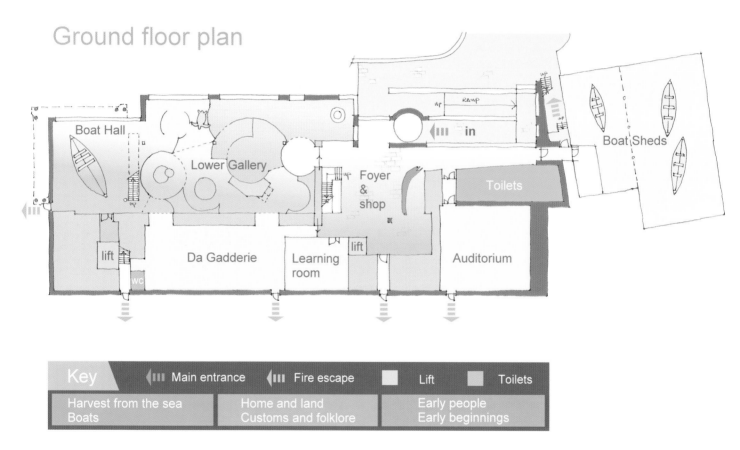

Until around 1800 Shetland was isolated.
Change came slowly, and islanders had
their own traditions.

After 1800 ideas, people and goods moved in and out of Shetland. Change came rapidly, and Shetland life became cosmopolitan.

Upper floor plan

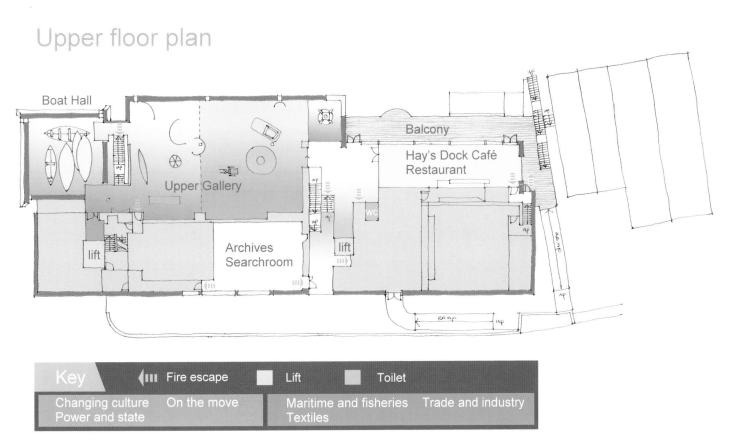

Boat Hall

Balcony

Hay's Dock Café Restaurant

Upper Gallery

WC

Archives Searchroom

lift

lift

Key	◀‖‖ Fire escape	■ Lift	■ Toilet

Changing culture	On the move	Maritime and fisheries	Trade and industry
Power and state		Textiles	

BOATS

> *An open boat, only 22 feet keel, having on board a quantity of potatoes, oat meal, five horses, a foal, a cow, some pigs, and 23 grown up persons and one child. We landed on the Fair Isle in 7 hours from Sumbro.*
>
> *Rev. John Lewis | 1824*

The Barracoutta was one of the first 'maid' class racing boats to use a modern sailing rig. She won many trophies in the 1960s.

Boats have always been vital to life in Shetland. People used them to catch fish, and to travel around the islands.

Thousands of boats were imported from Norway in kit form, and were assembled by people in Shetland. Shetlanders had little wood to build their own boats. The trade fluctuated before stopping completely in the 1860s. After that time wood was imported from Scotland. Shetlanders began to build their own boats, developed from the old Norwegian designs. Many contemporary Shetland names for boat-parts are derived from Old Norse.

Skilled boatbuilders, with basic tools, served communities throughout Shetland. They worked outdoors, and built vessels by eye rather than using drawn plans.

Fourareens (four-oared boats) were the commonest type, used inshore and between the islands. The larger sixareen, a six-oared boat with one sail, had a crew of six men. These boats would go 40 miles or more to the far haaf, the deep sea fishing grounds. There, lines were set and the boat lay at the lines overnight waiting for the catch.

Men in Dunrossness and Fair Isle developed boats called yoals, long, light supple craft for fishing near the shore. These boats had to be small enough to be hauled on to the beach by their owners.

Boats didn't just take men to the fishing grounds. Until the 1950s open boats were the most convenient way of moving people, animals, peats and goods. Boats became

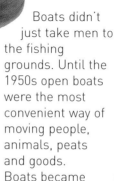
Sixareen crew men carried their food on board in small wooden Norwa bösts.

Landing fish at Sandsayre fish drying beach, Sandwick. The beach supervisor is directing operations.

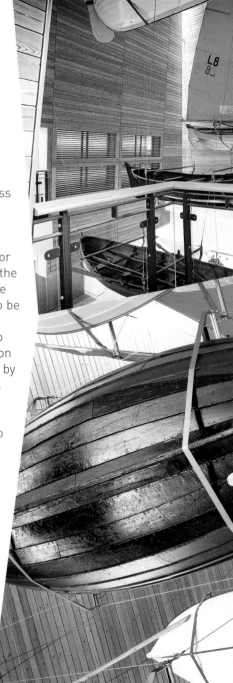

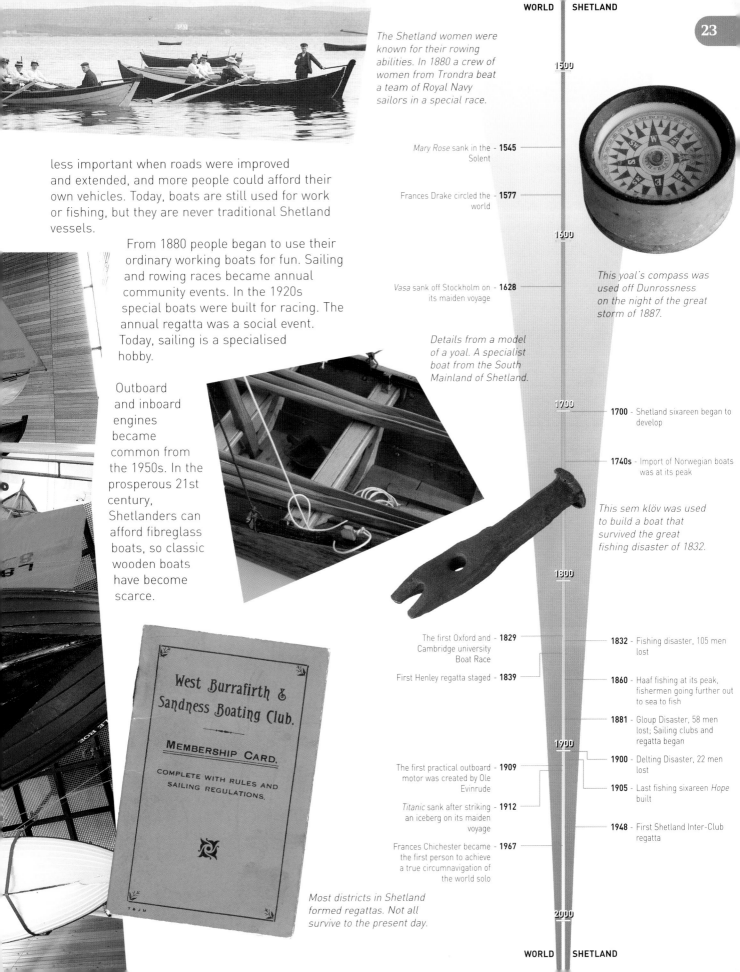

less important when roads were improved and extended, and more people could afford their own vehicles. Today, boats are still used for work or fishing, but they are never traditional Shetland vessels.

From 1880 people began to use their ordinary working boats for fun. Sailing and rowing races became annual community events. In the 1920s special boats were built for racing. The annual regatta was a social event. Today, sailing is a specialised hobby.

Outboard and inboard engines became common from the 1950s. In the prosperous 21st century, Shetlanders can afford fibreglass boats, so classic wooden boats have become scarce.

The Shetland women were known for their rowing abilities. In 1880 a crew of women from Trondra beat a team of Royal Navy sailors in a special race.

This yoal's compass was used off Dunrossness on the night of the great storm of 1887.

Details from a model of a yoal. A specialist boat from the South Mainland of Shetland.

This sem klöv was used to build a boat that survived the great fishing disaster of 1832.

West Burrafirth & Sandness Boating Club.

MEMBERSHIP CARD.

COMPLETE WITH RULES AND SAILING REGULATIONS.

Most districts in Shetland formed regattas. Not all survive to the present day.

WORLD | **SHETLAND**

1500

Mary Rose sank in the - **1545** Solent

Frances Drake circled the - **1577** world

1600

Vasa sank off Stockholm on - **1628** its maiden voyage

1700

1700 - Shetland sixareen began to develop

1740s - Import of Norwegian boats was at its peak

1800

The first Oxford and - **1829** Cambridge university Boat Race

First Henley regatta staged - **1839**

1832 - Fishing disaster, 105 men lost

1860 - Haaf fishing at its peak, fishermen going further out to sea to fish

1881 - Gloup Disaster, 58 men lost; Sailing clubs and regatta began

1900

The first practical outboard - **1909** motor was created by Ole Evinrude

Titanic sank after striking - **1912** an iceberg on its maiden voyage

Frances Chichester became - **1967** the first person to achieve a true circumnavigation of the world solo

1900 - Delting Disaster, 22 men lost

1905 - Last fishing sixareen *Hope* built

1948 - First Shetland Inter-Club regatta

2000

WORLD | **SHETLAND**

CHANGING CULTURE

> ❝*I am sure the Hall and Reading Room will be the greatest comfort to Burra, that it will be the scene of many a strenuous political conflict and of many a social gathering.*❞
>
> *J. Cathcart Wason M.P., at the opening of the Burra Hall | 1905*

From around 1800 new government policies and improved communication links meant that islanders were drawn closer to the rest of Britain. Social movements from outside Shetland began to influence and transform life in the islands.

The economic position of many Shetlanders began to improve. The old relationships between tenant, laird and merchant started to change. From around 1820 men left to work on whaling boats or serve on merchant ships and from the 1870s women often moved to mainland Britain to enter domestic service. The increasing prosperity of the islands eventually benefited the general population, rather than just the wealthy.

The German sailor toy must have brought a smile to a child.

Studying natural history was another hobby for the well-to-do. Visiting experts came here to find species that were rare elsewhere in Britain. They were also attracted by Shetland's unique plants and animals, which had evolved here because of the islands' isolation. Some local people, both rich and poor, also knew their district intimately and Shetlanders made important discoveries about their islands' wildlife. But only those with money could publish their findings, so many local collectors went unrecognised.

From about 1900 more people had paid jobs and fixed working hours. With spare money and time they could also take part in leisure activities. At home they made woodwork models and listened to the gramophone; outside they took photographs and went to the cinema.

Sport and recreation clubs were set up, especially in Lerwick. People played golf and tennis, sailed model yachts, debated and sang in choirs.

Portrait by John Irvine of Lerwick. He was Shetland's first Associate of the Royal Scottish Academy.

Two hundred years ago most Shetlanders didn't take part in sport and leisure activities. Only the wealthy had enough money and spare time for hobbies. Well-off families could buy equipment for sports and hobbies, and pay fees to join clubs. Since they had more free time, rich people could develop creative skills like painting and writing.

Wealthy Shetlanders employed maids to do much of the day-to-day work around the house.

DAVIS'S EXCELSIOR
WITH THE LATEST IMPROVEMENTS
LONDON

Up Helly Aas take place in winter throughout Shetland. A Viking longship is burned and squads dress up in fancy dress. This is the "Britannia" Up Helly Aa squad from 1914.

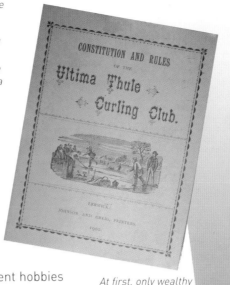

Cycling clubs enjoyed excursions around the islands. Shetland competed against sports clubs from Orkney and Faroe, both at home and away.

The increase in prosperity and free time during the twentieth century means that Shetlanders today have a large choice of different hobbies and things to do. The islands now have well-equipped leisure centres, built by the community to promote healthy living. There are public halls where folk meet to dance or for social evenings.

Insect trap from a wealthy home. Honey was poured inside this vessel and flies attracted to the sweetness quickly became stuck.

At first, only wealthy people had time to spend on hobbies.

MUSIC MUSIC MUSIC

Traditional fiddle music declined in popularity as listening to recorded music increased from the 1920s. In the 1950s, traditional music became commercially available for the first time. Since then Shetland composers and musicians have been inspired by local and international styles leading to a constantly evolving folk scene.

Tom Anderson is credited with preserving what remained of Shetland's traditional fiddle music.

Timeline

1500

1700

1800

Formation of United Kingdom - **1801**

Babbage invented first computer - **1835**

Queen Victoria came to the thone - **1837**

Phonographic recording device patented - **1857**

Charles Darwin wrote *On the Origin of Species* - **1859**

1822 - Walter Scott's *Pirate* appeared after his visit to Shetland

1827 - All twelve parishes had legal schools

1837 - Youths began to haul burning tar-barrels through Lerwick at Yule

1872 - *The Shetland Times* published

1873 - Up Helly Aa began

1900

Vacuum cleaner first invented; Queen Victoria dies - **1901**

BBC formed - **1922**

The Jazz Singer, first "talkie" picture, was made - **1927**

1913 - Lerwick's picture palace opened

First space flight - **1961**

1977 - Colour television arrived

1981 - First Shetland Folk Festival

1985 - Clickimin sports centre opened

2000

ON THE MOVE

Between 1770 and 1860 there was a steady increase in the Shetland population. This was largely due to the thriving fishing industry. However, from the 1870s until the 1960s, following changes in economy and society, the population fell. During this time many Shetlanders found life hard in the rural areas, and moved to Lerwick or overseas to look for work.

In 1886 Betty Mouat from Dunrossness, aged 60, drifted alone to Norway, when a member of the boat's crew she was on was washed overboard. The remaining crew left the boat in a launch to rescue him. They then couldn't catch up with the vessel.

James Robertson of Yell was famous for producing the first accurate map of Jamaica.

The desire for greater prosperity and a better life saw people look to far-away places. Colonial governments welcomed settlers, and agents advertised in Shetland for emigrants with farming and fishing skills. Some emigrants became rich, others fared less well, but many were better off than they had been in Shetland. Communities of Shetlanders grew up in places like Edinburgh, Wellington in New Zealand and Boston in the United States. They sometimes formed societies to keep their connection with the islands alive.

Within the islands there were changes in the way people moved around. Before roads were built people used boats as their main form of transport. During the famine of the 1840s a government agency paid men and women to make roads. As time passed people began to clamour for a road for their township: if they didn't get one they moved out.

The roads made it far easier for Shetlanders to transport goods to every corner of the islands. This changed Shetland's industrial life. From around 1910 motor transport made Shetlanders even more mobile. Nowadays industries depend on road transport to get materials and workers in or out.

Communication with places outside Shetland also improved. From the 1840s a regular postal system connected Shetland to the rest of Britain, and in the 1860s a telegraph cable made contact with the mainland even easier. In the early twentieth century communications improved again when the telephone and later the wireless (radio) came to the islands.

North of Scotland Company paddle steamer St Magnus I.

> **"Over-crowding is still very bad in many districts.
> This could be considerably redressed by the
> abolition of box-beds."**
>
> *Duncan Macarthur, Sanitary Inspector | 1896*

There have been increasingly regular links between
Shetland and the mainland since 1800. From the
1870s people became more and more dependent
on shipping from the south to bring them the
goods they wanted, and to export their products.
Today air travel means that Shetlanders can reach
the mainland quickly, and both people and freight
come here on the 'north boat'.

*The arrival of oil and
increased vehicle
traffic, encouraged the
local authority to
introduce inter-island
ferries. This model was
used to demonstrate
the principle.*

We now rely on external links for
everyday survival. Nearly
everything we own
or use comes by
boat: flour for our
bread, the clothes we
wear, the tools we use.
When the service is
disrupted, even for 24 hours, it
can cause panic buying in supermarkets.

With increasing numbers of people living in towns
and villages there was a demand for better
conditions. In the mid nineteenth century Lerwick
got its first gas supplies, as well as public
sewerage and water schemes. Electricity followed
in the 1920s. Small villages clustered round a shop
and post office became common throughout
Shetland. Water and electricity schemes eventually
came to these areas too. This meant that people
could stay in rural areas that they might otherwise
have deserted.

*The Orkney and
Shetland American
was published to
keep exiles informed
of events at home.*

*The many gates on
Shetland roads were
an annoyance to the
motorist. But to
children opening them
it was a good source of
holiday pocket money
from grateful drivers.*

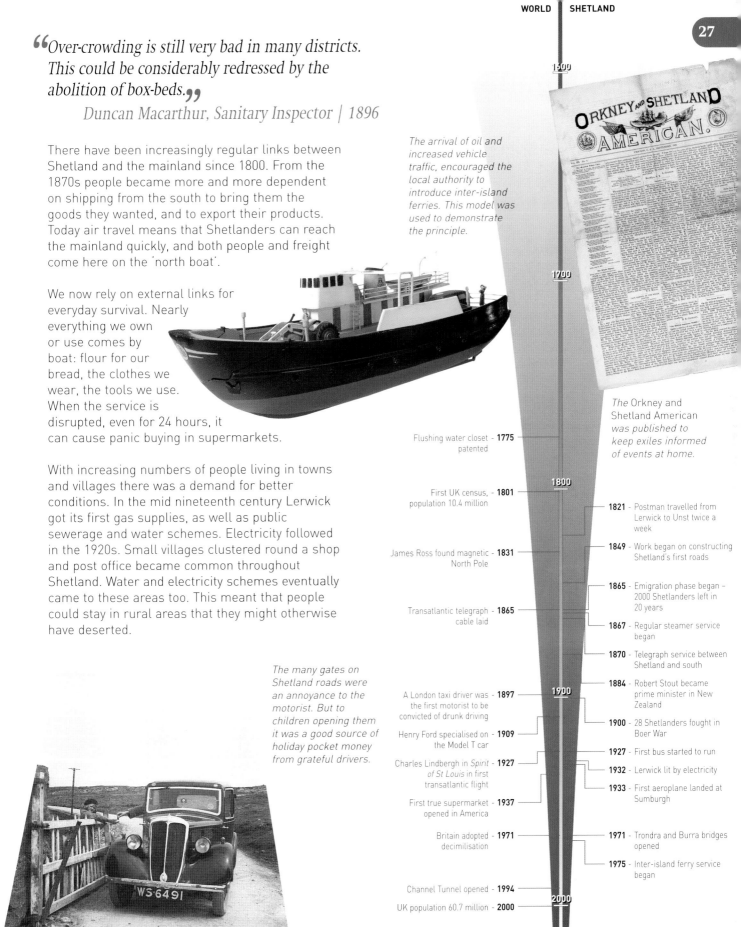

World

1600

1700

Flushing water closet - **1775**
patented

1800

First UK census, - **1801**
population 10.4 million

James Ross found magnetic - **1831**
North Pole

Transatlantic telegraph - **1865**
cable laid

1900

A London taxi driver was - **1897**
the first motorist to be
convicted of drunk driving

Henry Ford specialised on - **1909**
the Model T car

Charles Lindbergh in *Spirit* - **1927**
of St Louis in first
transatlantic flight

First true supermarket - **1937**
opened in America

Britain adopted - **1971**
decimilisation

Channel Tunnel opened - **1994**
UK population 60.7 million - **2000**

2000

Shetland

1821 - Postman travelled from
Lerwick to Unst twice a
week

1849 - Work began on constructing
Shetland's first roads

1865 - Emigration phase began –
2000 Shetlanders left in
20 years

1867 - Regular steamer service
began

1870 - Telegraph service between
Shetland and south

1884 - Robert Stout became
prime minister in New
Zealand

1900 - 28 Shetlanders fought in
Boer War

1927 - First bus started to run

1932 - Lerwick lit by electricity

1933 - First aeroplane landed at
Sumburgh

1971 - Trondra and Burra bridges
opened

1975 - Inter-island ferry service
began

POWER AND STATE

"A proposal has been made to start hot dinner for school children from a distance, but the scheme is not likely to be successful as only a very limited number of parents have expressed their willingness to let their children participate in it."

Bressay School Log | 1889

The increasing influence of the state has been both good and bad for Shetland. The state became the provider of health and education services, but government actions also affected people's lives in less welcome ways.

Lerwick Town Council made regulations about many aspects of life in the town.

As well as national government, Shetland was administered by a system of local councils. For most of the 19th century there was one council for Lerwick and another for the rural areas. At first the councils had little power as they had little money. Councillors were generally wealthy men such as merchants, doctors, lawyers and shopkeepers, and they sometimes used the councils to serve their own interests. Over time elections were held and councillors became more representative of the wider community. Nowadays Shetland Islands Council has powers in a wide variety of areas, from transport to culture.

The Church had a major impact on people's lives. The kirk session (local committee) was made up of the minister and elders of the Church. It enforced standards of behaviour within the parish. The session also played an active part in local affairs,

such as education and social welfare. Up to the 1820s the Church of Scotland was the only denomination. After that time other denominations, especially Methodism, became popular. As these functions became the responsibility of government, the Church became less powerful and its influence declined.

The Church, and individuals, provided schooling until 1872, when compulsory state education was introduced. Schools were then built across Shetland and education was free for everyone. Children from better-off families could go to the Anderson Educational Institute in Lerwick, and might go on to university or college outside the islands. Nowadays there are fewer, but larger, schools, where a broad range of subjects is taught.

The Rev James Ingram built the first Free Kirk in Shetland. He infamously banned the playing of the fiddle in Unst.

From the 1880s efforts were made to improve the health of islanders. New hospitals appeared in Lerwick and greater numbers of doctors and nurses were employed throughout the isles. In 1948 the National Health Service was introduced, providing free healthcare for all.

"Goliath" by Adam Christie 1935. Adam was from Cunningsburgh and at the age of 32 was sent to the asylum at Sunnyside, Montrose. He never returned home and over the next 50 years became renowned for his stonework and carvings of animals and heads.

Young criminals were often sentenced to be thrashed by the birch. This birch, from 1830, has been well used and has lost about one third of its size.

WORLD | SHETLAND

Wireless set used by the Norwegian resistance during WWII. The movement of soldier, spies and equipment to Norway became known as the Shetland Bus.

Nurse and patient at Montfield tuberculosis hospital. Patients were given plenty of fresh air and rest as part of the treatment.

Buckle, from the shoulder belt of the Lerwick Infantry 1798-1816. Lent by National Museums of Scotland.

Some of Shetland's dealings with national government were not to Shetland's benefit. Three major wars brought increasing disruption to the islands.

During the Napoleonic Wars thousands of Shetland men were captured and forced to join the British Navy and fight far away from home.

During World War One combat was more intense, having greater effect on those at home. At first men were patriotic and signed up willingly. Following heavy losses, however, there had to be conscription.

The Second World War directly affected Shetland and the impact on the home front was even greater. Not only men, but women too, were in the forces. In all these conflicts more Shetlanders served on the sea than on the land.

This tin was given to troops on the first Christmas of the First World War. It contained chocolate and cigarettes. Non-smokers normally swapped cigarettes for chocolate and other goodies.

Timeline

WORLD

- Napoleonic Wars began - **1793**
- Top hats worn in public for - **1797** first time
- Battle of Trafalgar - **1805**

- William Booth founded - **1865** Salvation Army

- Röntgen received Nobel - **1901** Prize for discovery of X-rays
- Men over 21 and women - **1918** over 30 given the vote

- National Health Service - **1948** created
- Last British execution - **1964**

- Dolly the sheep cloned - **1997**
- Scottish Parliament - **1999** founded

1500
1700
1800
1900
2000

SHETLAND

- **1795** - 3000 seamen in navy from Shetland
- **1845** - Organised poor relief
- **1858** - First gas lighting of Lerwick streets
- **1862** - Anderson Educational Institute built by Arthur Anderson
- **1872** - Education Act provided education for all
- **1879** - Rev Ingram of Unst died at the age of 103, the oldest minister in the world
- **1884** - Lerwick Town Hall opened
- **1890** - Zetland County Council formed
- **1901** - First general hospital opened
- **1910** - Lerwick's new post office was opened
- **1918** - End of World War 1 – 618 Shetland dead
- **1945** - End of World War 2 – 357 Shetland dead
- **1975** - Local government was reorganised. Shetland Islands Council (SIC) came into existence

WORLD | **SHETLAND**

TEXTILES

Jan. 3, 1872. 183... *Mrs. Arcus.* ...market ...them wo... market, ... 1833. here?—I... began. T... I was very...

"The class that strikes the eye so forcibly is the well-known Fair Isle hosiery. The startling brilliancy and variety of hues claim attention at once, before one has had time to notice the patterns carefully. The colours are bright yellow, brick red, marine blue, and white, with here and there touches of brown and green." — Weekly Welcome | 1897

Socks and plain woollen goods were the mainstay of the Shetland knitwear industry until the rise in popularity of Fair Isle in the 1920s.

For at least 150 years Shetland has been renowned for its distinctive and beautiful textiles. These range from fine-spun knitted lace, colourful patterned knitwear, to woven tweed.

Initially, the whole process from sheep to garment was done by hand. The preparation of yarn was often a social occasion, but was also a very skilled job. Wool from native sheep was carefully sorted and carded (brushed) into rolls, which were made into yarn on a hand-spindle or spinning wheel. If colours were needed, dyes were made from local plants or from imported substances. Some yarn for lace knitting was bleached to make it white. Finished garments were washed, stretched and dried.

Lace knitting originated in the 1830s. Knitters in Unst specialised in this type of work and gained a very high reputation for the extremely fine lace they produced. The work was time-consuming and garments were aimed at the luxury market outside Shetland.

Going golfing in the 1920s.

Despite the skill and labour involved, women received little reward for their work. Until the 1870s, knitting was sold to local shopkeepers, who gave goods such as tea or paraffin in return. Shopkeepers then sold the garments on to companies on the British mainland and made

substantial profits for themselves. These companies marketed Shetland goods to growing urban markets. Knitters' families couldn't avoid debt when things became difficult and women had to return with more knitwear. This method, known as Truck, was investigated in 1872.

A pair of cairds used to comb the wool so it lies in one direction prior to spinning.

Early knitwear designs were often plain, but as early as the 18th century, travellers to Shetland noted the colourfully patterned knitwear. These multi-coloured patterns called Fair Isle became popular, and their production eventually spread to the rest of Shetland. During the 1920s Fair Isle designs became very fashionable and the Fair Isle jumper was often associated with sports such as golf and tennis. Sometimes knitwear manufacturers used the words "Shetland" or "Fair Isle" to sell their products even when they had no connection with the isles.

NEW Knitting No 19
WOMEN'S
Fair Isle

A lace edging of very high quality.

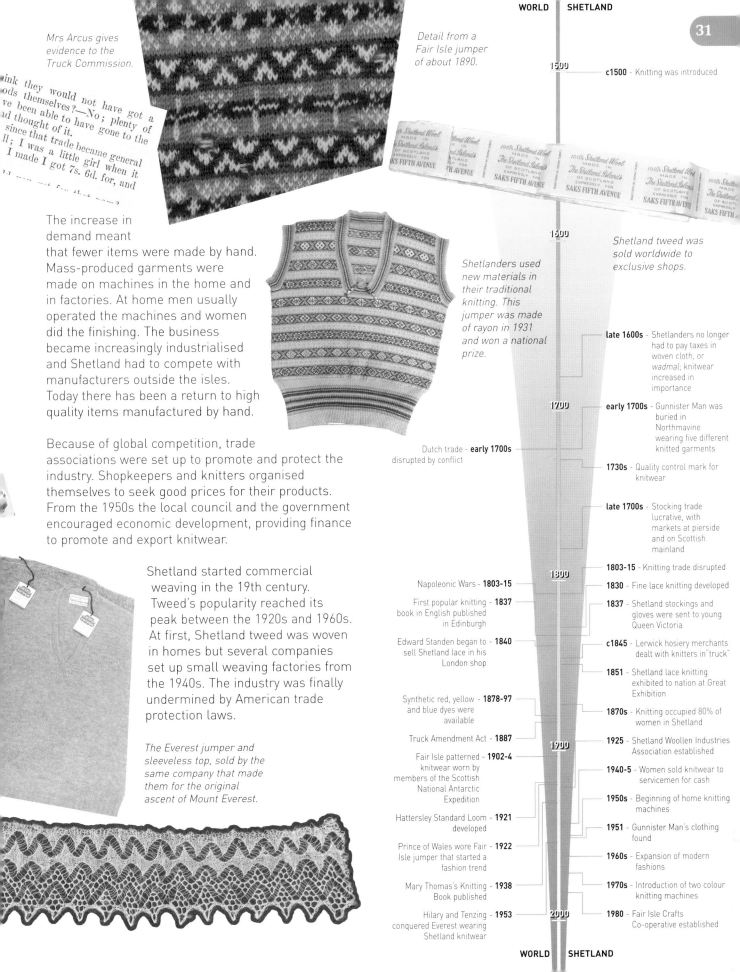

Mrs Arcus gives evidence to the Truck Commission.

ink they would not have got a ods themselves?—No; plenty ve been able to have gone to the ad thought of it. since that trade became general ll; I was a little girl when it I made I got 7s. 6d. for, and

Detail from a Fair Isle jumper of about 1890.

The increase in demand meant that fewer items were made by hand. Mass-produced garments were made on machines in the home and in factories. At home men usually operated the machines and women did the finishing. The business became increasingly industrialised and Shetland had to compete with manufacturers outside the isles. Today there has been a return to high quality items manufactured by hand.

Because of global competition, trade associations were set up to promote and protect the industry. Shopkeepers and knitters organised themselves to seek good prices for their products. From the 1950s the local council and the government encouraged economic development, providing finance to promote and export knitwear.

Shetland started commercial weaving in the 19th century. Tweed's popularity reached its peak between the 1920s and 1960s. At first, Shetland tweed was woven in homes but several companies set up small weaving factories from the 1940s. The industry was finally undermined by American trade protection laws.

The Everest jumper and sleeveless top, sold by the same company that made them for the original ascent of Mount Everest.

Shetlanders used new materials in their traditional knitting. This jumper was made of rayon in 1931 and won a national prize.

Shetland tweed was sold worldwide to exclusive shops.

Timeline

WORLD | SHETLAND

1500

c1500 - Knitting was introduced

1600

late 1600s - Shetlanders no longer had to pay taxes in woven cloth, or *wadmal*; knitwear increased in importance

early 1700s - Gunnister Man was buried in Northmavine wearing five different knitted garments

Dutch trade - **early 1700s** disrupted by conflict

1700

1730s - Quality control mark for knitwear

late 1700s - Stocking trade lucrative, with markets at pierside and on Scottish mainland

1800

1803-15 - Knitting trade disrupted

Napoleonic Wars - **1803-15**

1830 - Fine lace knitting developed

First popular knitting - **1837** book in English published in Edinburgh

1837 - Shetland stockings and gloves were sent to young Queen Victoria

Edward Standen began to - **1840** sell Shetland lace in his London shop

c1845 - Lerwick hosiery merchants dealt with knitters in "truck"

1851 - Shetland lace knitting exhibited to nation at Great Exhibition

1870s - Knitting occupied 80% of women in Shetland

Synthetic red, yellow - **1878-97** and blue dyes were available

Truck Amendment Act - **1887**

1900

1925 - Shetland Woollen Industries Association established

Fair Isle patterned - **1902-4** knitwear worn by members of the Scottish National Antarctic Expedition

1940-5 - Women sold knitwear to servicemen for cash

Hattersley Standard Loom - **1921** developed

1950s - Beginning of home knitting machines

Prince of Wales wore Fair - **1922** Isle jumper that started a fashion trend

1951 - Gunnister Man's clothing found

1960s - Expansion of modern fashions

Mary Thomas's Knitting - **1938** Book published

1970s - Introduction of two colour knitting machines

Hilary and Tenzing - **1953** conquered Everest wearing Shetland knitwear

1980 - Fair Isle Crafts Co-operative established

2000

WORLD | SHETLAND

TRADE AND INDUSTRY

Agriculture changed in the 19th century as new ideas and technology came to Shetland. Farming became increasingly commercial and industrial.

Some landlords tried to change parts of their estates into large sheep farms which they thought would be more profitable than having tenants on the land. From the 1820s onwards families were made to leave their homes to make way for sheep. Land where crops had been grown for centuries became grazings.

In the end the early commercial sheep farms failed: the breeds they used were not suited to the harsh Shetland climate, and before the regular shipping service began in the 1860s it was difficult to export the animals. There were more clearances after 1886 when the Crofters Act was passed. This gave tenants protection from unfair rents or evictions.

Government schemes and new farming equipment also changed the way the land was used. New equipment meant that farming became less of a communal activity as fewer people were needed to work the land. Government subsidies and grants encouraged sheep production, and today the traditional balance between crops and animals has gone. Very few people grow grain or potatoes today.

People no longer made things themselves, but paid specialists to do it for them. Coopers, carpenters and masons had very physically demanding jobs. Others such as watchmakers, dressmakers and cobblers did intricate, time-consuming work mainly in their own homes.

Some tradesmen, especially stonemasons, travelled to do their work. Others had their own workshops, serving a local community. Unskilled labourers quarried and shifted stones for masons. Tinkers were tradesmen who came to Shetland each year to travel around the islands. They sharpened knives, made lanterns and repaired buckets.

From the left: Several dairies sprung up around Lerwick to supply the growing population. The bottle dates from c.1950. Local shops often produced souvenirs to sell to tourists. This cup is a set of six from around 1910. Tin of traditional soup manufactured in the 1950s did not catch on, as locals thought the soup tasted 'thin and tinny'! Shopkeepers branded bought-in whisky with their own labels c.1900.

"The times have changed, and we, without doubt, have changed with them. Now everything, or almost everything, is worked either by steam, or gas, or electricity or petrol."

Thomas Manson | 1923

The Shetland Bank was an integral part of the business of Hay & Ogilvy, Lerwick. It collapsed when the firm went into liquidation following the 1842 fishing collapse.

Rural areas had small shops and there were larger shops in Lerwick. Some of the bigger companies even had branches throughout the isles. Most shops sold everything from food to fuel to boots and jackets.

Tourists started to come to Shetland around 1800. At first only well off people could afford to come but eventually more and more folk were able to enjoy the scenery, wildlife and history of Shetland. Early tourists were catered for in hotels or boarding houses. Today glossy brochures entice visitors and they can buy Shetland gifts and souvenirs.

The discovery of North Sea oil in the 1970s caused enormous changes in Shetland. The islands became much more prosperous and many people found employment in the oil industry. The influx of oil money has meant that Shetland now benefits from good roads, schools and many other public amenities.

Around 1900 many hotels were built in rural Shetland to cater for the increasing tourist trade.

CLOUSTA HOTEL
BIXTER, SHETLAND

CHARMINGLY Situated at the Head of the beautiful land-locked Voe of Clousta. Shooting over 20,000 acres ; also, Seal Shooting on the coast in the immediate vicinity. Fishing for Brown Trout and Sea Trout in 18 lochs ; 20 to 30 lbs. Brown Trout, and 25 to 35 lbs. of Sea Trout for Day's Fishing.

GOOD BOATING, BATHING, & SEA FISHING

ROUTE—ABERDEEN to LERWICK or WALLS, thence drive. Arrangements have been made with Messrs. GANSON BROTHERS, Coach Hirers and Livery Stables (near Lerwick), to run a Coach to Clousta in connection with the Mail Steamers arriving in Lerwick, by which Visitors will be taken to the Hotel at a charge of 5s. each, exclusive of luggage.

Telegraph and Post Office, 4 miles

TERMS :—£3 per week for Fishers, except during August, September, and October, when the charge will be £3 : 6s. 10s. per day, except during August, September, and October, when charge will be 11s. Non-Fishers £2 : 10s. per week, or 8s. 6d. per day. Shooting and Fishing Free under those charges. Boats on all the good lochs at 3s. per week.

SPECIAL TERMS WILL BE MADE FOR FAMILIES

Visitors for this Hotel coming to Lerwick are recommended to the Grand Hotel there, the Manager of which will give them all further particulars in connection with this Hotel they may desire.

For further Particulars apply to J. C. GRIERSON, Solicitor, Lerwick, Secretary to the Proprietors.

Local cartoonist Frank Walterson accurately caught the crofter's early problems in handling the iron horse tractor.

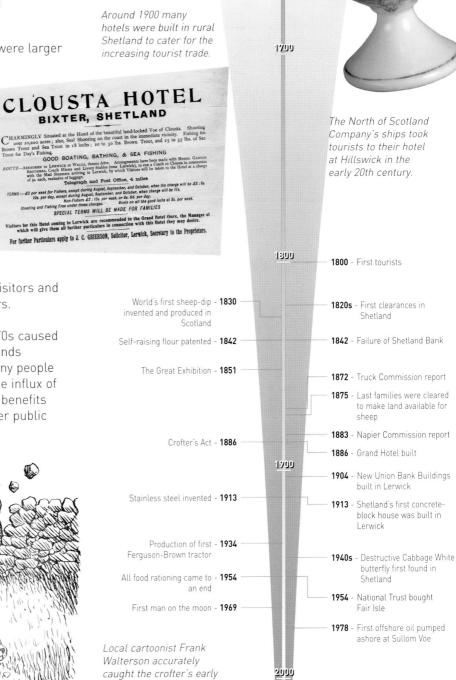

The North of Scotland Company's ships took tourists to their hotel at Hillswick in the early 20th century.

WORLD	SHETLAND

1500

1700

1800 — **1800** - First tourists

World's first sheep-dip - **1830** invented and produced in Scotland

1820s - First clearances in Shetland

Self-raising flour patented - **1842**

1842 - Failure of Shetland Bank

The Great Exhibition - **1851**

1872 - Truck Commission report

1875 - Last families were cleared to make land available for sheep

1883 - Napier Commission report

Crofter's Act - **1886**

1886 - Grand Hotel built

1900

1904 - New Union Bank Buildings built in Lerwick

Stainless steel invented - **1913**

1913 - Shetland's first concrete-block house was built in Lerwick

Production of first - **1934** Ferguson-Brown tractor

1940s - Destructive Cabbage White butterfly first found in Shetland

All food rationing came to - **1954** an end

1954 - National Trust bought Fair Isle

First man on the moon - **1969**

1978 - First offshore oil pumped ashore at Sullom Voe

2000

MARITIME AND FISHERIES

"For generations the "sea" has drawn young Shetlanders, not from any mystic charm or romance that may enshroud ships and the sea, but from the all-impelling economic reason to make a living."

Peter Jamieson | 1949

Shetland has always relied on the sea. Going to the fishing or sailing in the merchant fleet was a source of income for Shetland families. Working at sea also brought Shetlanders into contact with people and cultures from around the world.

In the 1880s a huge herring boom began and workers flocked to Shetland to catch and process the fish. Today Shetland's herring boats are the biggest in Britain and the fish is processed locally before being exported all over the world.

Hauling the catch on board the drifter Perseverance.

From the 1820s Shetlanders developed a new fishery, for cod. They abandoned traditional boat designs in favour of decked boats called smacks, and went as far afield as Rockall and Faroe. Besides cod the fishermen also took back smuggled alcohol. Haddock fishing was prosperous from the 1880s, and from the 1920s boats were motorised. The white fishery was revolutionised in the 1940s, when nets and navigation aids were adopted meaning that boats could catch much more. Due to declining stocks the fishery collapsed in the 1990s.

Many Shetlanders sailed to both the Arctic and Antarctic to hunt whales. The Arctic whale fishery began around 1770, based in ports on Britain's east coast. It was driven by the demand for whale oil, whalebone and other materials. Shetlanders were in demand because of their skill in handling boats. They earned good money catching the whales, flensing them (cutting blubber from the whale's carcass), and rendering the blubber (melting it down for oil).

Antarctic whalers painted faces onto sperm whales ear drums.

The demand for whales later saw whalers working in the Southern hemisphere. From the 1920s many Shetland men sailed to the Antarctic. They were often away for six months or a year at a time. The Antarctic whaling was an industrial operation, much like factory work. The workers earned a lot of money, which was very useful at home, but conditions were tough: a harsh cold climate, long hours of hard work, poor working conditions and dangerous machinery. Falling stocks meant that the whale fishery closed in 1963.

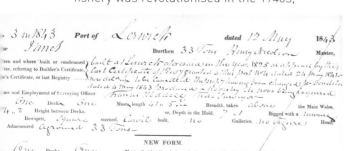

The Janet, a local merchant's ship, was registered in Lerwick in 1843.

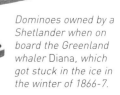

Dominoes owned by a Shetlander when on board the Greenland whaler Diana, which got stuck in the ice in the winter of 1866-7.

Dutch gin crook. Found in the stomach of a Fin whale being cut up at the Olna whaling station in 1905.

Britain once had the largest merchant fleet in the world. Ships brought materials from all over the globe, and took manufactured goods to the colonies. From the 1820s to the 1950s shipping companies employed large numbers of seamen. Many Shetlanders found work in this way as they were familiar with maritime work. They often became captains or mates – one of the few chances of "getting on" that people had. With the souvenirs they brought home – pictures, models, crockery, and toys – Shetland homes took on an international feel.

With time on their hands, merchant seamen often made toys and crafts for family back home, like these nodding parrots.

Although the sea has often been a source of livelihood for Shetlanders it has always been a dangerous place too. Shetland's rocky coast has always been a hazard for ships on the busy sea routes that pass close by. Islanders often risked their lives trying to rescue sailors from wrecks.

From the 1820s there were organised efforts to reduce the number of wrecks, and prevent loss of life. Coastguard volunteers kept watch from huts and were trained to use life-saving gear. From the 1930s an organised lifeboat service began in Shetland. Lighthouses were built around the coast from the 1820s, with fog horns to warn shipping when visibility was poor. Improvements in ship navigation, like accurate charts, radar, and satellite positioning, have also helped to make wrecks rarer.

Bell from the "silver ship" Wendela, wrecked on Fetlar in 1737 and subsequently used on a fishing station in Whalsay.

The refurbished Bressay lighthouse mechanism forms one of the corner-stones of the present building.

This figurehead came from the brig Elwine of Stettin, which was wrecked near Spiggie in November 1877, with the loss of all her crew.

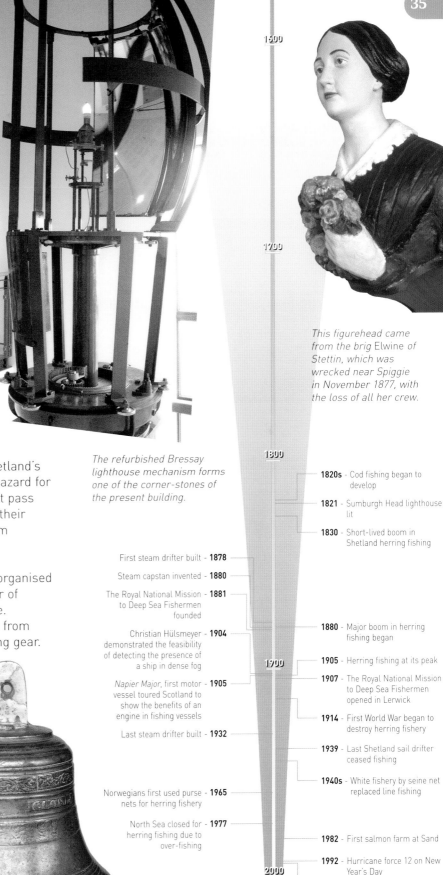

WORLD | SHETLAND

1600

1700

1800

1820s - Cod fishing began to develop

1821 - Sumburgh Head lighthouse lit

1830 - Short-lived boom in Shetland herring fishing

First steam drifter built - 1878

Steam capstan invented - 1880

The Royal National Mission to Deep Sea Fishermen founded - 1881

1880 - Major boom in herring fishing began

Christian Hülsmeyer demonstrated the feasibility of detecting the presence of a ship in dense fog - 1904

1900

1905 - Herring fishing at its peak

1907 - The Royal National Mission to Deep Sea Fishermen opened in Lerwick

Napier Major, first motor vessel toured Scotland to show the benefits of an engine in fishing vessels - 1905

1914 - First World War began to destroy herring fishery

Last steam drifter built - 1932

1939 - Last Shetland sail drifter ceased fishing

1940s - White fishery by seine net replaced line fishing

Norwegians first used purse nets for herring fishery - 1965

1982 - First salmon farm at Sand

North Sea closed for herring fishing due to over-fishing - 1977

1992 - Hurricane force 12 on New Year's Day

2000

1993 - Braer disaster

WORLD | SHETLAND

TEMPORARY EXHIBITIONS

One visit to the Museum and Archives isn't enough! We have a running program of changing temporary exhibitions, displays and events. The main space for exhibitions is Da Gadderie on the ground floor. This flexible space was named by competition and means a gathering of various things.

Exhibitions in Da Gadderie are art, craft or artefact based. They usually change each month, in connection with relevant local and national events, and reflect four categories:

- 'Made in Shetland' features individual and group shows by artists and makers permanently resident in Shetland.
- 'Made for Shetland' highlights the work of national or international artists or makers.
- Touring exhibitions comprise exhibits of national and international significance.
- Finally, there are exhibitions curated by the Shetland Museum and Archives staff which, where possible, relate to local or national cultural events.

We are is always keen to hear from people who would like to use Da Gadderie for an exhibition or event.

Details of how to apply can be found on the web site at www.shetlandmuseumandarchives.co.uk or ask to speak to the Exhibitions Officer.

A contemporary textile display inspired by two knitters from the 1930s.

Uniquely within the permanent displays there are a number of cases specifically designed for changing. These are called "focus displays" and allow the Museum and Archives team to focus on a particular object, theme or new donation that relates to the zones on display.

The Learning Room and Auditorium both host small exhibitions and paintings can be seen in the upper foyer outside the Café Restaurant.

A temporary exhibition on Admiral Fraser's court uniform.

Da Gadderie can be configured to suit different exhibition needs.

LEARNING AND EVENTS

Artist workshops, family days, craft demonstrations and tours are just a few of the events that happen at Shetland Museum and Archives. You'll find something for all ages and interests. Events relate to the collections and the changing exhibitions in Da Gadderie.

Events are held throughout the building from storytelling in the Boat Hall, to demonstrations in the galleries and boat sheds. The Auditorium is used for films, lectures and conferences. Collection-based and artist talks also happen within the galleries and Da Gadderie.

As well as informal learning events the Shetland Museum and Archives has a busy education service. Tours, workshops and resources have been developed to meet the needs of learners of all ages and abilities. Events range from tours for pre-school pupils, to workshops for secondary school pupils and allow pupils to learn about Shetland's past.

Schools and community groups can also borrow from the popular Discovery Box service. The boxes contain artefacts on particular themes such as Crofting, and are used for everything from reminiscencing, to art and drama. Staff regularly visit schools and groups on outreach visits, to show artefacts and give talks.

A range of workshops are held which focus on arts and crafts or research methods. You can learn how to research a family, boat or business or whatever takes your fancy. You might also want to make a clay pot with your child or learn a new textiles skill. Workshops occur in the learning room or archives searchroom, but book your place fast as they are very popular.

PUBLIC ART PROJECT

More than 60 pieces of art, by local, national and international artists and makers, are displayed both inside and outside the building. Ranging from intricate textiles and new pieces using indigenous crafts to new media and films, each piece was made specially for the Shetland Museum and Archives.

On the dock the Shetland Receivers broadcast fragments of conversations, songs, whisperings and voices about Shetland life. In the Archives handmade wooden panels depict notable historical themes including emigration, and the clearances. The inlays in the tables at the Hay's Dock Café Restaurant are equally fascinating. In the foyer, the reception desk has been crafted from the remains of the *Elenore von Flotow*, a ship discovered under the mud in the dock.

THE MUSEUM SHOP

The shop is the perfect place to buy a souvenir of your visit to the Shetland Museum and Archives.

As you browse the shelves, you will discover a wide range of gifts, many locally made, that reflect our collections, including jewellery and clothing, books, postcards and keepsakes for all ages. Friendly staff will offer advice on your purchase.

HAY'S DOCK CAFÉ RESTAURANT

Upstairs you can enjoy the relaxing atmosphere of Hay's Dock Café Restaurant.

The 50 seat licensed Café Restaurant specialises in providing high quality, fresh and healthy dishes that showcase the very best of Shetland's produce whenever possible.

Hot lunches, as well as snacks, cakes and excellent fair-trade coffees are available during the day. In the evening diners can enjoy the chef's contemporary Scottish cuisine in a more relaxed atmosphere.

Children are more than welcome – we can provide baby chairs, heat up baby food, and provide smaller cutlery if required. Please advise the staff of any special dietary requirements so that the kitchen staff can accommodate them accordingly.

Hay's Dock Seafood Chowder – serves four hungry people

500g mixed whitefish, preferably sustainable breeds such as pollack, ling, catfish (some can be smoked)
225g tatties (potatoes), peeled and chopped into random sizes
75g chopped leeks
1.2 litres water
150ml double cream
Green peas to taste (frozen)

Boil the tatties until they are soft. If the tatties are different sizes, some will be mushy and some will still have some bite which is good. Add the leeks and cook for 10 minutes so the green parts still have colour. Add the fish chopped in to chunks and simmer for five minutes. At this point, season the soup to taste with salt and white pepper and add the peas. Simmer for a couple of minutes, then add the cream and serve garnished with chopped parsley or dill and perhaps a pinch of nutmeg. Delicious!

SHETLAND CROFTHOUSE MUSEUM

The thatched house and outbuildings, typical of the late nineteenth century, provide a fascinating insight into how Shetland families lived at that time. Beyond the house, there is a byre, barn and mill.

The building, which is three miles north of Sumburgh on the A970, is open from mid-April to the end of September. Admission is free, but donations are welcome to help maintain the house. Unfortunately, due to the nature of the building, it is unsuitable for wheelchair access. More information is available from the custodian on 01950 460557 or the Shetland Museum and Archives on 01595 695057.

BÖD OF GREMISTA

The Böd of Gremista, at the north end of Lerwick (past the power station), is the birthplace of Arthur Anderson, co-founder of what became P&O Ferries. The building is an example of a typical late eighteenth century böd (booth), which provided family accommodation as well as a working store for the nearby fish-drying beach. Some rooms are restored in period style, while others have displays on a maritime theme.

The Böd of Gremista is open from early May until late September and admission is free. Wheelchair access is limited to the ground floor and the steepness of the stairs may limit access to people with disabilities. For more information contact the custodian on 01595 694386 or the Shetland Museum and Archives on 01595 695057.